SMART MONEY CONC

AN INSIGHT TO TRADING LIKE BIG BANKS

AND INSTITUTIONS IN THE FINANCIAL MARKET

THE SMC INSTITUTIONAL ORDER BLOCK, BREAKER BLOCKS, BREAK OF MARKET STRUCTURE, LIQUIDITY SETUPS, LIQUIDITY POOLS, STOP HUNTS, CHOCH, MITIGATIONS, SUPPLY AND DEMAND

Michael Giovanni

DISCLAIMER

This book is not a financial advice; it is only intended for educational reasons. Trades are entered at the risk of the trader as this book does not provide a 100% guarantee. However, when studied and put into practice, it will greatly aid you in understanding and enhancing your trading adventure. It's recommended for traders to get knowledge from a variety of sources to assist them become better traders. Before making any financial decisions, consult a certified financial or investment advisor. Regarding the claim made here, the author disclaims all warranties. So please trade responsibly at all times.

AN INTRODUCTION TO SMART MONEY CONCEPT, AN INSIGHT OF HOW THE BIG BANKS AND INSTITUTIONS TRADE THE FINANCIAL MARKET.

When a large trader or institution takes a large position in a particular asset or market, its actions can have a significant impact on the supply and demand dynamics, leading to changes in price and market direction. For example, if a large institutional investor decides to buy a significant number of shares in a particular company, this can lead to increased demand for the shares, driving up the price. Similarly, if a large trader takes a short position in a particular market, this can lead to a decrease in demand and drive the price down.

Strong Low (SL)
When the price broke market structure was high. The low point becomes a strong low. Strong Low is The Low that caused Manipulation and Break Structure (resistance).

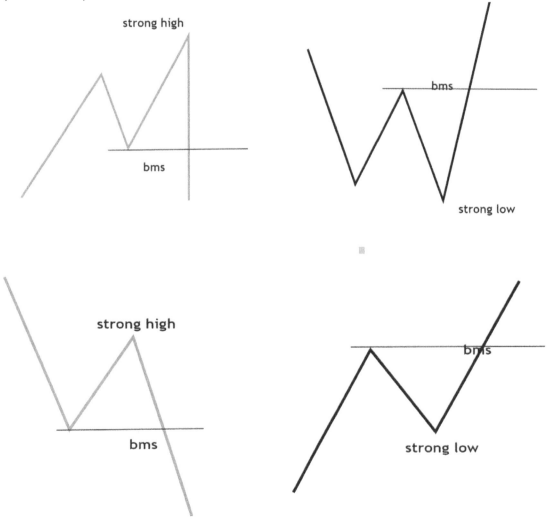

In an uptrend, there was a new high, and in a downtrend, a new low. Weak High or Low is produced always from a strong High or Low. Weak Low/High is the Low that fails to break structure.

For a very strong LOW, there is a weak High

Every every strong High, there is a weak Low

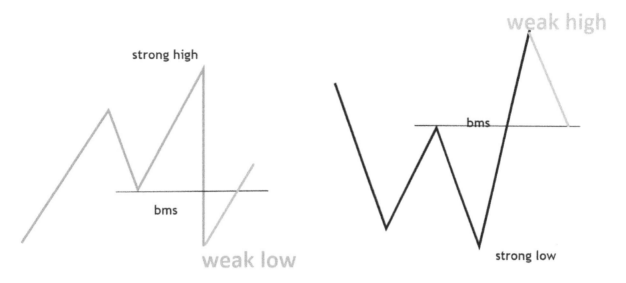

Break of Market Structure

Any time a candle breaks and closes outside of the structure (swing high in an uptrend and swing low in a downtrend), it is referred to as a structural break. In other words, the previous structure has been destroyed, and a new one has been formed. Break of the structure created by a continuing trend.

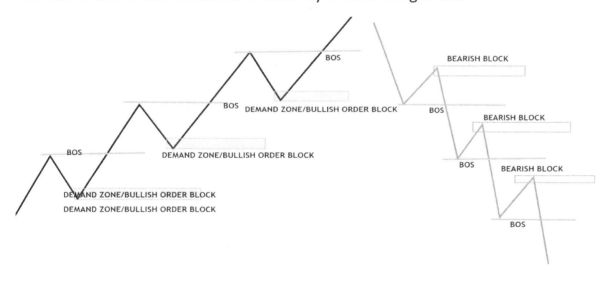

Identifying Potential Order Blocks

Once the market structure has been broken, traders may look for potential order blockages. The traces the market makes following a sudden activity are called order blocks. The last opposing candle before a large move that disturbs the market's equilibrium is known as the Order Block (OB). After determining the market, the next step is to find substantial bullish or bearish order block zones. These are regions where the balance between supply and demand is considerably out of whack. Depending on the higher period trend, look for a bullish or bearish order block (for instance, if the trend is down, seek for a bearish order block; if up, look for a bullish order block).

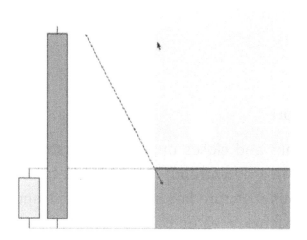

When Does Supply and Demand Break?

Supply and Demand levels eventually break when a zone is repeatedly tested or during a significant change. Due to a large quantity of orders in the other direction breaking the level or the remaining orders being triggered and gradually withdrawn.

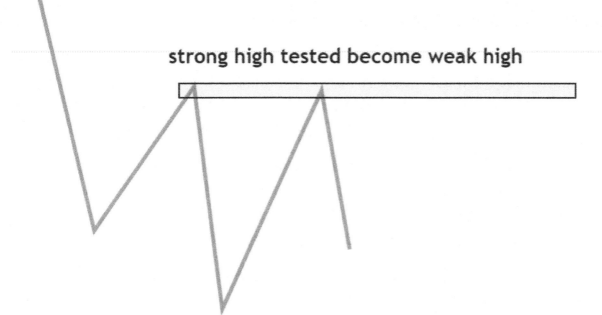

strong high tested become weak high

THE SMC BULLISH AND BEARISH ORDER BLOCK

How Smart Money Concept and Order Blocks Work

It's the final candle before the hasty decision that destroys the edifice. Essentially, this means that the most recent HH or LL is eliminated. If neither an HH nor LL is formed nor the price moves upwards or downwards, the final candle is not recognized as a legitimate OB; a valid OB requires that the price break structure.

We are more likely to see the unexpected price reaction we are looking for in an untested supply and demand zone or OB than in one that prices have already entered to offset. This is what I mean when I say that when examining supply and demand, or Bullish and Bearish OB, the newer is typically better.

An OB's 50% equilibrium point serves as a broad guideline for when price tends to moderate before continuing in that general direction. According to my own testing, if a price is paid to fill 50% of the OB, we can now state that the OB has been mitigated and finished, and further searching for the possible interest area is not necessary.

It's important to think about the timeframe you're trading on as well as the current market structure you're watching.

If so, it will make more sense to look for long trades at demand zones and short bearish OBs than it will to look for supply zones and short bullish OBs.

Naturally, the same concept also applies if your market structure is bearish.

In general, the more significant the zone is to the HTF, the greater relevance the OBs will have, increasing their significance and reliability. Taking a long, for instance, from a 4h or 15m OB that only caused a $500 price change.

Bullish Order Block

A bullish order block is the final downward candle that precedes a bullish impulsive move to the upside that breaks structure. Strong rising momentum will accompany this move, which often leaves some price imbalance in its wake.

The supply and demand levels where important institutions have made substantial market purchases are known as order blocks. Theoretically, pricing will ultimately return to this order block to fill any liquidity, rebalance price, and permit the placement of more orders.

Since they typically leave imbalance behind once we acquire this OBs shape, pricing must first stabilize and improve before rising higher.

We can find a certain entry point and stop loss using OBs. Enter at the top of the OB with a stop loss at or just below the OB.

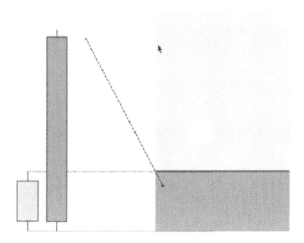

This figure demonstrates that this OB is bullish because there is a BOS and the momentum can enter on the subsequent candle.

The price moves toward the OBs where more orders can be placed to maintain the bullish trend in order to fix any leftover liquidity or imbalance.

With these OBs, we may arrange an entrance so that whenever we impulsively move away, we can place the OB just below, our stop loss at the low, and our entry at the top of the OB. We can position it a few pip below if we have some wicks or if we allow for a small surge.

Bearish Order Block

A bearish order block is the last candle that is up before a bearish, impulsive move to the downside that upends structure. Strong downward momentum will be present, which usually results in some price imbalance.

The idea is that because major institutions have made sizeable orders in this area of the market, prices will eventually return to these OBs. to make new orders, change the price, and fill any available liquidity.

Before prices may start to fall, these OBs must return and become efficient since once they develop, they often leave imbalances behind.

We can recognize a distinct entry in OBs and stop loss. One should enter at the top of the OB with a stop loss at, or slightly below, the OB.

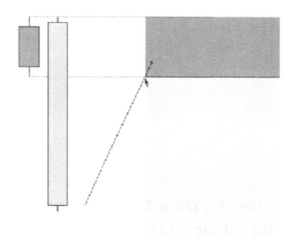

One thing we could do with all the OB would be to filter it down and see where momentum had entered the market if this was our OB and there was a candle that followed it but didn't engulf the true OB. We can concentrate on the bullish or bearish candle instead of the most recent upward or downward movement.

Refinement of Order Block

If possible, we can really reduce the OBs, thus it's critical for us to pay attention to where the most recent momentum has entered the market. for instance, the entrances of the institutions. Price movement is possible because it must first go back to the point where the momentum started before moving forward.

Refining our OBs is advantageous since tightening our AOI enables us to enter more accurately with a larger stop loss and often minimizes our draw down to our trade. Additionally, it will provide us the chance to increase our trade's return rate, which will increase our return. The instances that follow show how OB has improved. This means that, as can be seen, the bullish OB gave us a final downward movement, which was followed by a brief bullish candle that didn't engulf the OB or provide us any clues about the direction of the trend. The motion was actually seen in the candle that came next. In order for us to concentrate on this bullish candle as our OB.

We have exactly the same circumstance with the bearish OB to the right.

Bullish Order Block

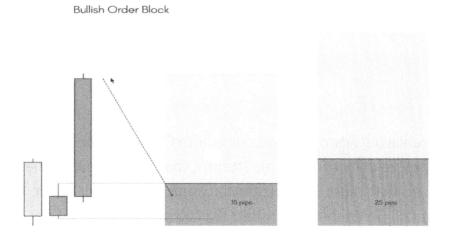

This will serve as our opening bid (OB), but as you can see, a bullish candle followed it. Pay attention to the fact that it doesn't seem to be signaling any momentum or market movement, though.

That momentum hasn't been shown because it hasn't closed above the OB. In fact, the candle that came after it showed that this candle was swallowed by momentum. We may thus use our OB, which is situated here and denotes the most recent downward move, as our OB.

We can tighten our stop loss, reduce drawdown, and increase return on investment (RR) on our trades if we cut our AOI by -10 pips. As an illustration, the RR on this candle is 15 pip, as opposed to 25 pip if we could have stayed to this OB.

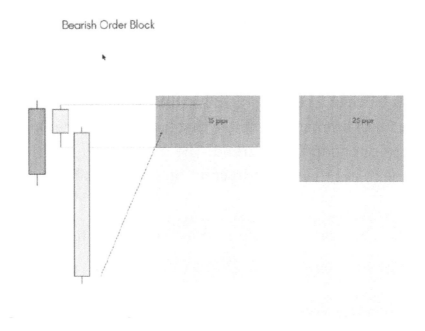

The only difference between this and our bullish OB is that the candle that followed did not show any velocity or make an attempt to engulf the OB. When we focus on this, you can see that there is a substantial amount of momentum. It follows that this is now our OB. Given that the initial OB is 25 pips and the refines stop loss is 15 pips, which includes the wicks, it is prudent to provide some leeway for price movement by positioning the stop loss above or within the wick.

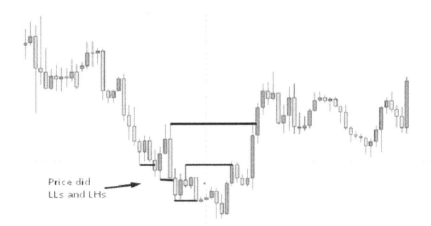

We shall now discuss other OB and refinement examples. We are at the 1h on EU, and looking at price activity, we can see that we were before in a fall. For this reason, it is evident that we are adding LLs and LHs.

As a result of the altered market structure, we BOS upward before backtracking and destroying this high. We are looking to add HHs and HLs because it is clear that we are currently in a bullish trend.

Therefore, we begin looking for suitable longs as soon as BOS is trending upward.

Last down candle, but next candle was the last candle before the impulse move to the upside

If we look to see where the OB will be, we can see this final downward movement before to the impulsive upward movement of the BOS. The BOS pushed back as we pushed up. The fact that the candle after this OB is present and has not yet devoured this candle shows that momentum has not been proven. We can elaborate on this further, but this is the OB.

Therefore, we can actually refine it, and when we refine down OB, it won't always mean that the AOI is tighter; instead, it means that we can be more accurate. However, in this instance, the wick is big, thus this is our OB; generally, it will be tighter.

Since there are still price disparities, an imbalance basically exists whenever either buyers or sellers seize control without providing the opposing party a chance to respond.

You can see that there will be an imbalance from one wick to the next since they do not meet, which suggests that there will only be buyers inside.

It follows that the price will rise again in the future to correct the imbalance it caused before possibly continuing to do so.

As you can see, as soon as we impulsively stepped away, the price began to adjust. In fact, the price didn't return to our OB because we held EQL on an LTF when we swept the liquidity from EQL. But what exactly did it achieve? Will it eventually result in the mitigation of the majority of this imbalance—not all of it—before proceeding?

This will occasionally take place even if we don't get a tap into the OB because it frequently simply rebalances any liquidity or imbalance from just above the OB.

We are aware that an order might have been placed here even if we weren't tapped. An order would have been positioned below the wick or at the top of a refined OB.

Therefore, we may set this entry and have a 12 pip stop loss in place after the structure has been broken.

Since it is unlikely that the price would increase further now that the imbalance has been fixed, we may close the trade as soon as the price BOS this structure.

We are aware that no structural integrity has been harmed as we press forward from this point. To allow for liquidity above this EQH, we just wicked up this high and created this EQH.

Now that this is our OB, we may place an entry by pricing this EQH and leaving an OB. We are unable to refine that entrance down as we did here, though, because this was the final downward movement and the candle that followed it signaled the start of momentum.

Due to our large stop loss, we may actually drop to an LTF in this example and attempt to modify it.

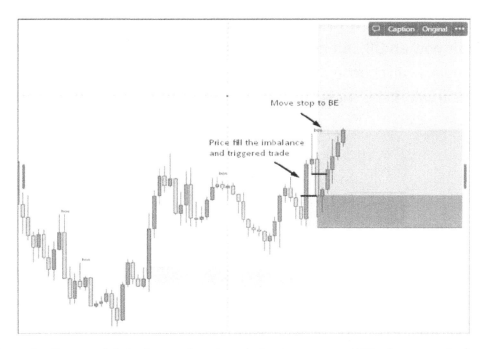

The price decline, which is easier to detect on an LTF, is now balancing the effectiveness of this upward rise. The anticipation is that the price will continue to reach higher highs despite the fact that we have mitigated, which means that more purchase positions have stacked close to the sell positions.

We were activated and tapped into this commerce; it is what we do. Below this wick is where our stop loss is.

Due to the price's recent formation of a new BOS, we can move our stop loss to BE.

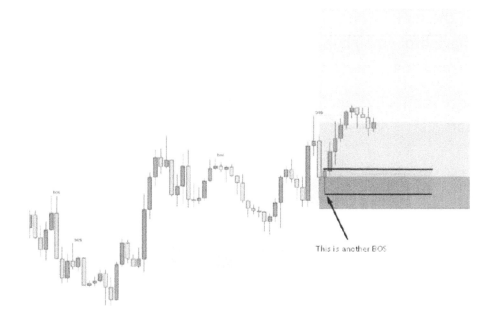

Will I be looking at the downward swing that started the transaction now that we have BOS? It is now an OB, but it is extremely large, so we may refine to this candle. For this example, I will choose this candle because it shows some momentum even though there aren't many wicks, but we did push off BOS.

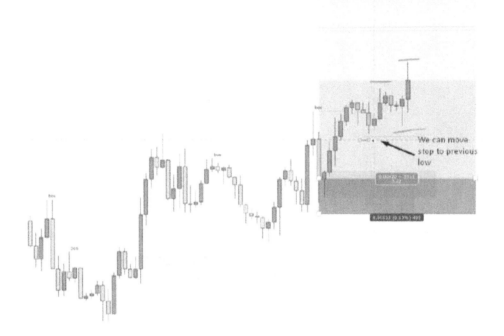

Since the price movement is effective and does not require more decline to improve the situation, I would not be looking to enter a trade at this time or consider this to be an OB.

If we were in the initial trade, we may try to lock in more profit at this bottom because we have broken higher. If we were successful, we would push up, as we had predicted, and begin inserting these HHs and HLs.

As a result, price is effective and correcting, therefore I wouldn't be trying to make any scaling trades.

Thus, as the price made BOS to the upside once more and left an OB, which is the candle in our case, we put a limit order at the base and a stop loss below it. At this time, price had created an imbalance, so we could anticipate a price down to fix it before prices started to increase again.

Therefore, before starting our transaction, we must first correct this imbalance.

2

SMART MONEY CONCEPT ENTRY TYPES

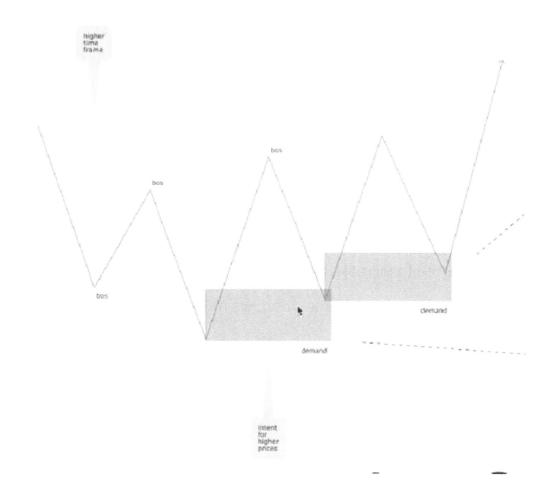

When looking at the HTF, it may be the daily, 4 hours, or 1 hour, but I utilize the 1 hour period as my highest because it gives me a lot of opportunity and is simply a great timeframe to sort of base our trades on. Now, whether you select the daily or the 4h as your peak periods relies on your particular tastes. But if we look at this figure, we'll find that it's an HTF; for that reason, we'll call it the 1h.

Once we obtain a bullish OB (POI), we can clearly detect a change in momentum, and as we can see, bullish order flow follows. Prior to being pushed upward and BOS, the price first dropped.

An OB or demand level exists inside of the BOS now that it exists. Therefore, I think that when price first starts to trade in this zone, there is not enough confluence for us to set a pending limit order. There won't be enough convergence once the price is set, so I won't even think about going long. Before verifying an LTF for our entrance confirmations, I'd rather wait for the price to be provided and see how it is delivered. Many SMC traders would classify that kind of entry as a risk entry, but I personally don't want to risk losing money, especially when we are trading with substantial sums of cash. I would rather wait to see how the price moves into that range because I have had far better success doing so. I would then search LTF for our entries. I won't be looking at any risk entries because of this.

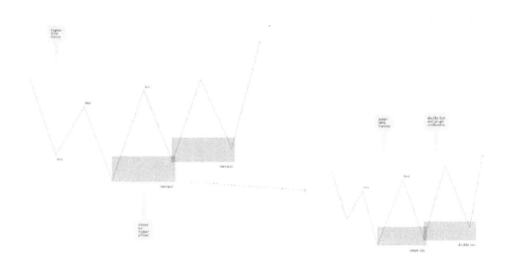

As a result, if we get here, this will be the initial amount of demand, as we can see if we look at the different kinds of submissions. We are therefore looking for longs at this kind of demand level. On an LTF, this would seem as thus right now. As a result, this will be our LTF. As for me, I execute transactions on a 1m, occasionally plunging into the 30s. But we'll continue to use 1 m.

As a result, as the price drops and moves into this region, an LTF frequently exhibits LLs and LHs.

As a result, before looking for indications of bullish action, we will wait for price to push in. So, we want to see a strong BOS. This would then give us access once it constructed an OB down here.

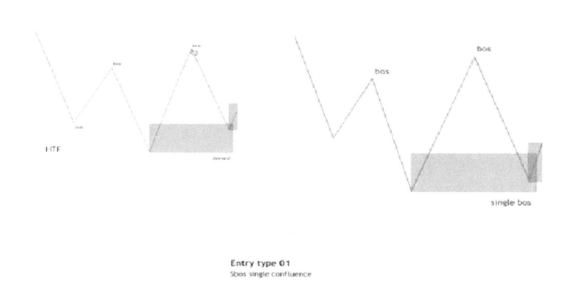

Entry type 01
Sbos single confluence

The entry type 1 for this trade is a single BOS, which essentially means a single BOS and a single confluence, as we can see on 1h, which is the first BOS on an HTF. Given that there is just one confluence and one BOS on the LTF, it is possible that this was a downtrend in the past, with the prior BOS indicating intent and tapping into a level of demand.

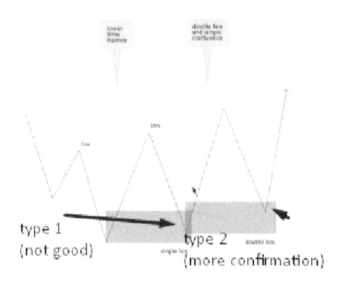

Entry type 2
Dbos single confluence

Entry type 2 would then be anticipating the double BOS, which is essentially a BOS that has the potential to pullback and then BOS once again. It is not necessary to reduce this level here.

I still view that as a double BOS because we are still trading at this 1h demand level and there is double confirmation on an LTF. A single confluence also exists.

Therefore, I would strongly urge you to avoid this entry (type 1) if you have difficulties entering trades or you take too many losses because when the price breaks now, depending on how it breaks plainly, it might just be a fake out before moving lower.

It depends on how it breaks, but there isn't too much proof. I'd suggest waiting for a double BOS if you're having difficulties with entries because we'll enter some stronger trades while we wait for more confluence. Additionally, we're beginning to see bullish order flow on our LTF, and the 1h demand level indicates that people appreciate us.

Price is trading above this lows

Entry type 03

Sbos double confluence

As a result, when entry type 3 is available, we will examine this second demand level on HTF. We moved back so we could see the BOS, and then we BOS. As a result, our order flow and clear bullish intent are both visible on the HTF. We can see what we accomplished now that the caption intent for HTF prices has been added. To put it simply, this indicates that prices had been trading above these lows, and that once this structure was broken, prices started to go higher. After pulling back, we surged upward once more, and now that prices have been unable to move below this level, it is obvious that we are signaling a desire for higher prices. When we go back to the third entry, we can see that there is a second BOS on 1h, which makes this a double confluence because it relates to our second demand level. We are simply seeing more confluence, which will keep prices moving upward.

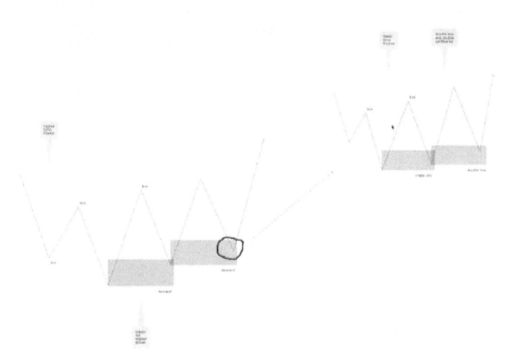

Now, here is how the pullback to the second demand level will seem or how we anticipate seeing it in order for the trade to comply with our entry requirements.

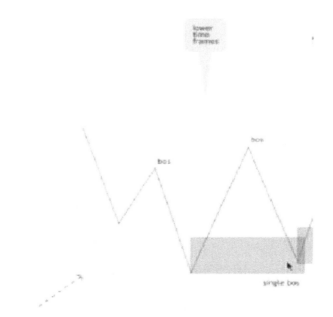

They are currently trading inside the second BOS and second demand level as a result.

As we can see, the price is already trading back into it, and LLs and LHs will also be present. As we trade in the second demand, we want to wait for a great BOS, which would be our single BOS but with two confluences.

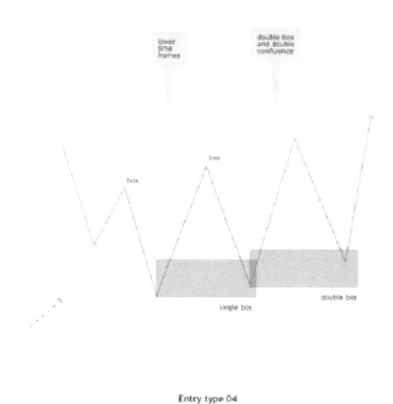

Entry type 04
Dbos double confluence

Entry type 4 demands that we wait for a double BOS now that we can witness one BOS, a pullback, and a second BOS. There are two BOS and two confluences as we trade at this second demand. While we will make some excellent transactions if we wait for this, we won't always make the trade. Type 4 is extreme and requires a great deal of confirmation.

Therefore, I do accept trades with a single BOS and a single confluence as long as we are trading with the trend. However, we will need to undertake testing on that because I also take a double BOS. However, it all depends on how it breaks. Nevertheless, as I previously stated, the absolute minimum that we should be taking is a double BS followed by entry types 3 and 4. After going through these continuation trades, it is imperative to recognize that they are only hypotheses and textbook setups. They won't always be this organized. As a result, we ought to use our initiative and think about what the price is actually doing.

How is the price trend?

What is the most likely cause of the price response?

Check for our entry from there since this is a continuing trade. Therefore, as soon as we start noticing HTF bullish or bearish order movement, like this, we want to look for the BOS.

Where are the supply and demand levels?

Where does the momentum start before the BOS?

So, where did the price increase that caused the BOS start?

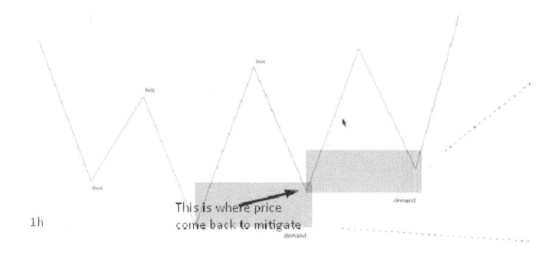

Since here is where price is likely to return to lessen the damage before continuing, it is essential to understand where price broke from and where the move began.

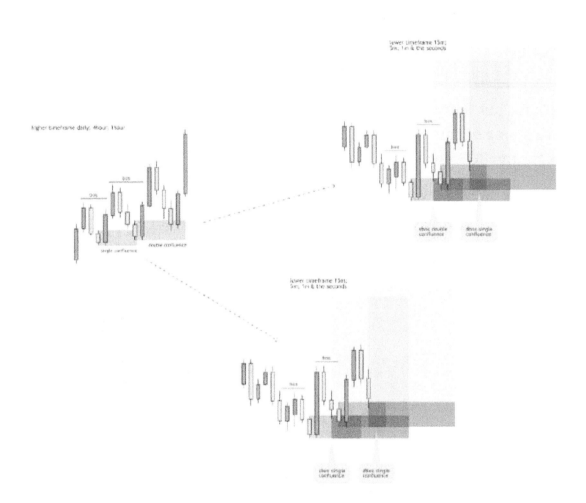

3

LEARNING ABOUT THE LIQUIDITY SETUP

Simply expressed, liquidity refers to how simple it is to enter and remain in a market at the right price, depending on the number of buyers and sellers present.

The market maker's primary objectives in terms of liquidity are:

1) To earn income by buying and selling from their own inventory when there are no public orders to buy or sell the item.

2) To maintain the market book of orders, which is made up of limited buy and sell orders as well as stops placed by participants in the general market.

In general, you can understand how the MM lures and deceives retail traders if you can understand these two fundamental concepts.

Order stops Part A of liquidity (BSL)

The BSL is a set of buy stop orders with corresponding stop losses.

The market turns lower when the BSL is removed (and the buy stops are activated), clearing the stop orders.

Identifying BSL

1) PMH (Previous Month High)

2) (PWH) Last week high

3) Previous day high

4) High of the day

 5) Old High/Swing.

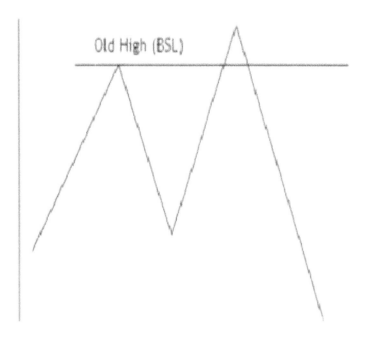

Old High (BSL)

B) Stops selling Liquidity [SSL]

The SSL is a collection of sell stop orders that each have a corresponding stop loss.

The market reverses to the upside and clears the stop loss orders when SSL is removed (sell stop activated).

Spotting the SSL

Previous Month Low (PML)

[PWL] Previous Week Low

Lowest Day Low [PDL]

High of the Day (HOD)

Equal Low [EQL] Support

Old Low / Swing Low

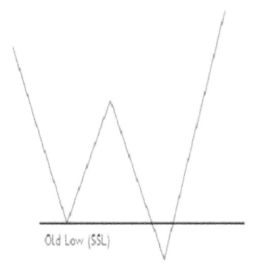

Old Low (SSL)

Market Liquidity Setup for Sharp Entry

We trade liquidity when?

Generally, should include the following.

a) Abandon Hunting [SH]

A hypothetical breakthrough above or below the region of liquidity is all that "SH" is.

b) Break in Market Structure [BMS/BOS]

A market that no longer maintains its structural integrity is referred to be BMS (HH or LL for a persistent trend; HL or LL for a direct change/CHoCH).

Liquidity Trading Considerations

a) Since the trend is your buddy, always trade in the direction of the HTF trend.

b) Demand and Supply: Consider market success and imbalance.

b) Support and Resistance [EQL EQH]: Always keep an eye out for fake outs in the SnR zones.

d) Understanding: If you enter the market after it has changed direction and suffer losses, this is the finest method for spotting a price retracement.

Example of Liquidity Setups.

1) SH – CHoCH with quick RTO (Quick Entry)

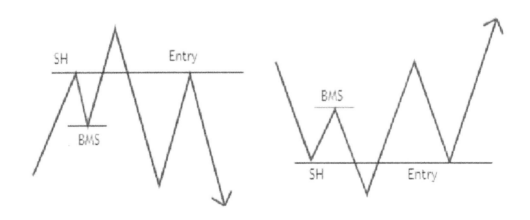

2) SH – CHoCH with late RTO

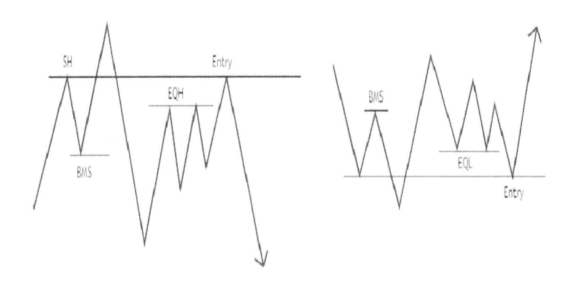

3) SH + Confirmation Entry (Re-entry) with quick RTO

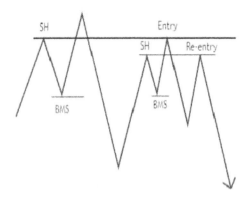 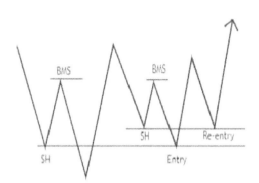

4) SH + Confirmation Entry (Re-entry) with late RTO

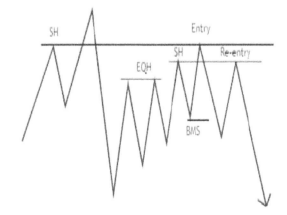 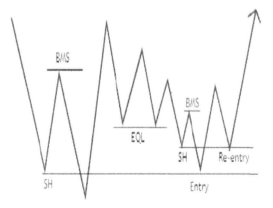

5) SH + Fake BMS

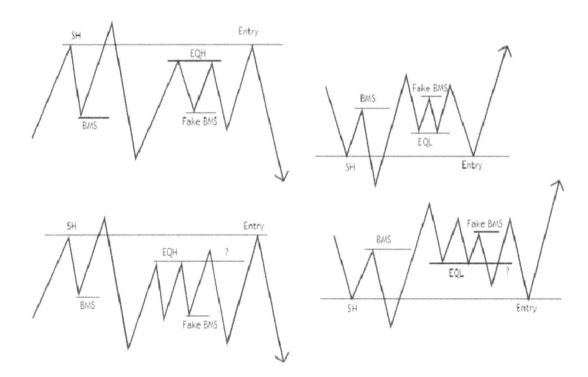

6) SH + Compression

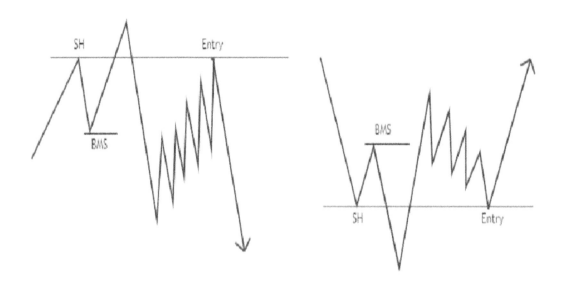

4

SMC MARKET STRUCTURE

Basic Market Structure Concepts

Understanding how a pair is behaving, what stage we are in, and when a pair structure is shifting direction requires knowledge of the market structure on a price chart.

So, is the tendency of a currency pair higher or lower? We are therefore including LLs, LHs, HHs, and HLs.

Can we move out? As a result, we aren't really moving up or down and are still within the market's two price points.

Is the price impulsive or corrective? Thus, by identifying the structure, we may ascertain what a pair is doing.

Therefore, like we just said, this market is moving upward. Therefore, in a market with an upward trend, we will see HHs and HLs. As a result, both a price decrease and an increase can be shown. This will definitely be the HL whenever the price breaks over this level. We won't have a distinct high-low until the price breaks through this high, so long as it stays above. We retreat HL as soon as we determine that HH is the most recent HL. Then, we keep an eye out for a new higher that confirms the HL, then the HH, HL, and HH structure.

The identical circumstance exists right now in a market that is declining, but it has obviously been reversed, making it the opposite. Thus, if the price doesn't move past this level, we will experience a low and a pullback. The break below verifies the LH, LL, retreat, LH, LL, and LH as a result of which. We might confirm an HH before we have a BOS of the most recent high, and the opposite is true for a downtrend.

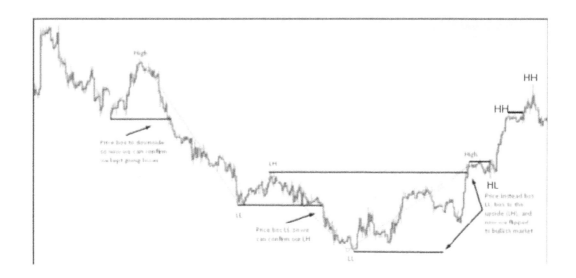

Now let's have a look at the EU charts. From this point forward, the price is pulled back, and since we've broken the trend line, we've established this low, which, as we might say, kept getting lower until it reached this level. There was a real slump at this moment.

Because of this, the entire leg below shattered. It has therefore obviously fallen to this low. So, an LL comes first, followed by an LH. As a result, we can see price reversal that draws from an OB, which would be more apparent on an LTF. Therefore, it is clear that the price has been dragged to its lowest point here, which needs to be broken.

The price has since retraced after one more leg to the downside, albeit this is not yet verified as an LH. But as we can see, the price tried to decline, but we were unable to do so, and instead, the price has risen to test the LH. After retreating, we finally break it with this hasty action that results in this LH. Our bias has shifted from being bearish to being bullish as a result of the LH being broken and the fact that we did not receive an LL.

It is obvious that the LH has been broken. When Price turned around, he gave us HH, which we can classify as the highest point. We can infer that this is a new HH because it broke over this highest point. Then we do the opposite and get an HH. This is the most recent HL as of at this moment.

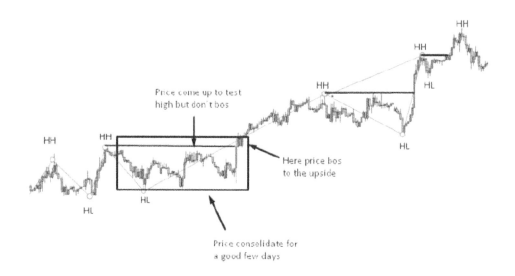

Price come up to test high but don't bos

HH

HH

HH

HH

HL

HL

HL

HH

HH

HL

Here price bos to the upside

HL

Price consolidate for a good few days

The price pulls back after reaching an HH and HL. The price climbs to test the high after a few days of consolidation, but it doesn't break it until now.

Where then would we put the HL? We can identify this as an HL because it is the lowest position in terms of technicality. This is only the HL, though, as there are places where we can witness growth sustaining itself for some time. Once we made the quick rise higher that broke this high, this was confirmed.

Next, we have an HH, in which the highest point is nearby; as a result, this is the most recent HL, HH, HL, HH. Now we can assert that the HH resulted from an impulsive move up that was afterwards reversed.

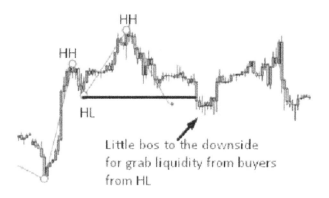

Little bos to the downside
for grab liquidity from buyers
from HL

We came down to test it, succeeded in doing so, and broke it afterwards, so we effectively gained a bit. However, since we didn't really tap into any form of POI, this may be folks who are long on this HL with stop losses grabbing liquidity.

Although this is the lowest place, we just pushed upward from there before placing an HH and an HL. We have HH after a BOS, which allows us to confirm our HL, which is always the lowest value. We now have an HL and HH once more. Although there are many BOS in LTF, this is the standard procedure for marking BOS.

Market Structure Mapping

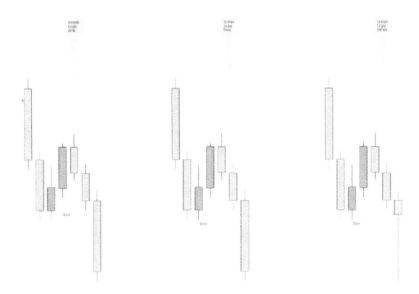

Several different kinds of market structure breaks are what I want to discuss.

Now, in order to proceed, it is essential that we choose and adhere to one of the following market structure breaks.

The first type will occur when the price breaks the structure with a candle body that closes below the candle body low because the wicks are not taken into consideration.

2. The second kind is a candle body that is near to the wicks of the candle, which is the most typical and what I myself use.

3. The third and last form is a candle wick that is situated immediately beneath the candle wicks. This type doesn't truly show a break, thus in my opinion it's the least likely to happen of the three.

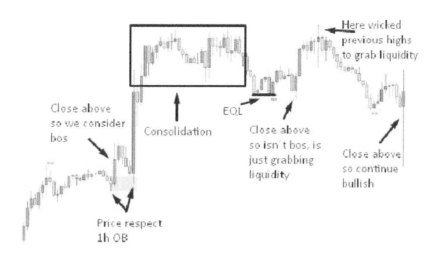

Close above
so we consider
bos

Consolidation

EQL

Close above
so isn't bos, is
just grabbing
liquidity

Here wicked
previous highs
to grab liquidity

Close above
so continue
bullish

Price respect
1h OB

Observing some BOS examples, we can see that on EU 1h, we had a BOS here, we had this higher, we had a small range, and then this candle broke structure, and we got a wick, but we did close above, and then we can see price pulled back into a bullish OB, which is here, before we see some pronounced momentum to the upside. Since we broke above and closed above the structure, I believe this is a legitimate type of trade to be considering as we enter this 1 hour OB, which we can further develop on an LTF.

But if we examine some of these instances, we can observe that there was a brief consolidation range, that range was pushed lower, that bottom was achieved, that low was surpassed and closed above, and that the price then reversed upward.

As we can see, we also get a wick above these highs before they reverse price up to these highs, which is taking some more buy side liquidity. Price then turns around, we record a new low, we pull back, and finally we have a massive wick.

The price moved below this level before closing above it at a point when we were bullishly closed.

In light of this, if we shift to the left, we also see that this wick perfectly mitigated before continuing by tapping into a bullish OB. Due to the fact that it is merely providing liquidity, rebalancing this impulsive move, and utilizing a bullish OB that has not yet been neutralized before the price reverses to the upside, I do not believe this to be a true BOS.

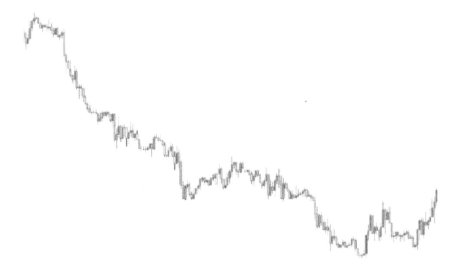

Another example is the 1hr EU, where we can be seen putting the LLs and LHs all in the way down.

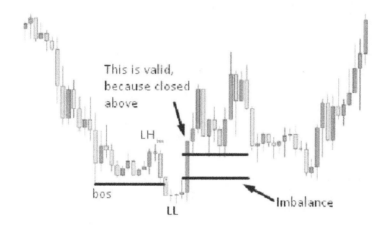

We can see that price was in this LL and LH at this point because this is the LL that broke this low here. It is evident that the price impulsively broke through the upward structure. I would classify this as a true BOS because we can see that the candle body closed over the wicks of this LH. Once we had this, we were able to see that we had also left a balance. This was a big shift that showed how the market's structure had changed.

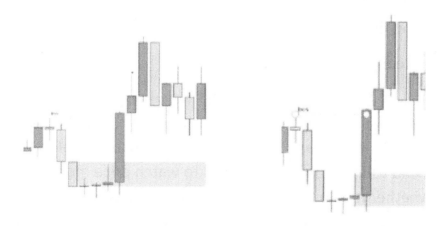

We can then refine our OB down to this candle using the most recent downward candle as our beginning point because momentum entered on the succeeding candle, which broke structure.

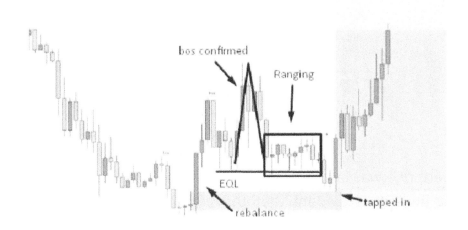

As you can see, following that, we did profit from a few days of range-buying, we repeated BOS, and now that we have done so, the price has fairly abruptly plunged into that level. It is more obvious on LTF that this is generating some liquidity. Given that we have EQL, we can examine how price behaved after entering our OB, which we can easily modify on an LTF, how price slightly rebalanced, and how price made the impulsive move to the upside from this point.

How does price break structure?

Now I want to look at how the pricing is determined. Therefore, when examining structure fractures, it is vital to pay attention to how a specific element of the structure is damaged. This means that I'll be breaking structural lows and highs, seizing liquidity, and using an unrestricted AOI to watch price move in line with the general trend, whether it be bullish or bearish. I'll be breaking structural highs and lows as an alternative. It is vital that we pay attention to how price breaks because it will give us a really clear idea of what price is actually doing and where it is going to behead.

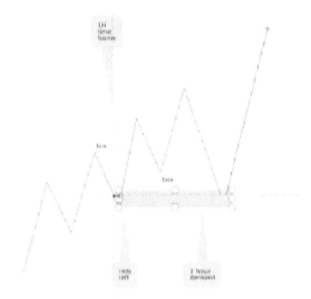

Here are some diagrams I've made in the first place. We can see that we have completely allocated this hour to HHs and HLs because it will be our first hour. Now, this action had broken the HL. The effect is that the structure is crumbling. For the purposes of this example, we'll suppose that this downward movement is a calm, corrective BOS.

Corrective BOS

There isn't much momentum behind it since it's just a BOS with corrective and low momentum candles.

When we make these HHs and HLs, we are breaking structures to the upside, creating demand levels and OBs. As a result, when this occurs, we will view it as a common corrective BOS, meaning it is very likely that the price is declining to sweep liquidity and tap into an unmitigated demand zone that was previously created. Any abandoned items might be shown, coupled with an untested, uncorrected imbalance. Due to this breaking pattern, anyone trading stop losses at the lows and in the bias may be losing liquidity. Every market low and high has liquidity, as we are aware.

This might be a BOS seizing liquidity by exploiting an unchecked OB to preserve the overall bullish bias.

In this situation, the cost would be equivalent to our hourly demand.

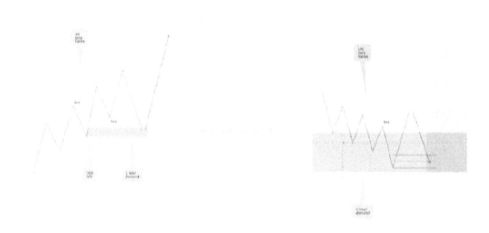

We can now know that this is a 1m viewpoint because we have an LTF. Therefore, the one-hour OB is this blue box over here. The move that descends that BOS on 1h will therefore appear like this on an LTF, allowing us to see LLs and LHs. When the price changes in response to the one-hour demand, we can search for where the LL and the LH are. We can monitor for price to move in a way that will result in a bullish OB from which we might think about getting long since we have an LL and this is the most recent LH. We may look for past one hour highs now that we have objectives since we anticipate seeing more bullish order movement. Due to the fact that we have swept liquidity, we want to see pricing put in fresh HHs.

Aggressive BOS

As a result, males who have HHs and HLs, which are the same as the corrected ones, will now act impulsively. The price imbalance that results from an aggressive BOS would therefore be indicated by some big momentum candles. After the price reaches its bottom, we may say that the market has turned bearish because of the significant momentum we have seen during this downward journey. Since we anticipate a retreat into that zone as well as additional LLs and LHs, the BOS, if we obtain it, creates a supply zone and OB from which we can consider going short. a downward flow of order.

For the purposes of this example, we're going to say that this is where we want to get short from once we get an impulsive BOS, albeit we may have spots underneath it that we can modify on an LTF.

When a result, if we take another look at it from the 1m perspective, this is what we might see when we use the 1h supply. Since this will provide us with an OB from which to short the market, when prices form HHs and HLs, we want to see a nice BOS below the most recent HL. Targets are the same way.

This 1 hour low is the most recent low that we want to see broken because our bias has changed from bullish to bearish, and we should at the very least be monitoring for price to enter LLs and LHs at that time. This is a good place to start your initial aim, at the very least.

Buy to sell

Let's assume that pricing shifts downward as seen here. We shouldn't be frightened to buy before the longer-term sell, whether that was a calm or aggressive action because it changed the structure.

We can still look to take longs from a certain spot if there is one to long from. A supply zone that has just recently created from this BOS to the downside can be the target if we have a demand level that hasn't been tested, depending on what the LTF confirmation is telling us as we approach it.

So, we buy from here and seek to increase our position before beginning a longer-term sell. We can expect the price to create new lows after that and then go on to lower and upper highs.

The shift from the supply to demand zone might be 30 pips, 20 pips, 60 pips, or whatever as we can use the LTF to our advantage going forward.

We can still make a significant percentage on this move before looking to sell. to purchase and sell. This has a larger likelihood because, if the price reaches this level, we are essentially neutralizing this move and taking liquidity from buyers or even traders who are trading some form of breakout in this structural break. Before they can see the price enter a supply zone, people are dispersed. Essentially, it creates space for liquidity so that the price can reach a supply zone and then shorten from there. Now that it has been neutralized and the demand zone has experienced a push off, we can say that this move is finished.

We have delayed until the price decreases. There is little actual reason to think that this demand zone will hold again because the effects of this move have already been significantly reduced. As a result, we can see price drops and low points.

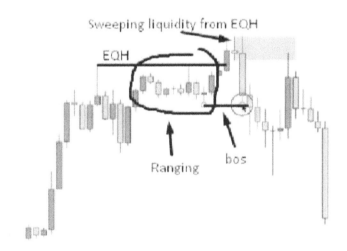

When we buy, we have the option to sell, after which we can hunt for a longer-term buyer from an unproven region. This is a situation of a sell to buy, or, more specifically, a buy to sell. I also made this deal as a result. As a result, relative to the price we had established as this high, there is a little bit of a variation.

We did develop EQH, and to maintain this level, some buy side liquidity was needed. So, when we had this high, we had an HL here. This is the HL because the transition broke to a new HH. After significant buy side liquidity, the price can be seen, and since the candle terminated below the BOS, it is a true BOS.

We can sell from this supply zone, before price come down to this candles here

On an LTF, such as the 15m and 5m, where we truly closed below, this can also be seen. Because it is a calm BOS and we have closed below, we can still try to sell from this supply zone before a longer-term buyer shows up from this area below. In my opinion, this would be best observed on the 1h, though.

Once we have the final upward movement prior to the downward movement that BOS, we can then refine it from this candle here since, as we can see, the candle has not yet ingested the OB. Therefore, we can attempt to go short from this supply zone and OB.

Take liquidity

As we descended, we did receive some wicks, which, in my opinion, did little more than draw liquidity from the HL that came before this one. Therefore, anyone holding from this uptrend and in a buy position would likely have stop losses at this low. You can see that the wick has lost its flame. There are obvious price decreases to absorb that reversed liquidity, then other price reductions. Consequently, it happens every day. As a result, after tapping in, we switch to an LTF and search for responses and BOS that leave imbalance. We can sell an LTF at this point. We must look left after tapping in OB to see whether there are any unchecked demand levels that have been left for a later time.

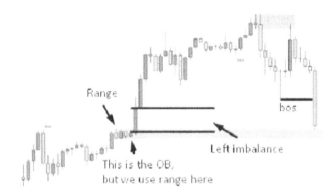

Let's look at it. This EQ was produced by an increase in both the HH and HL prices.

Then, we see a huge acceleration that successfully breaks this high point. We can identify it as BOS and wicked it in order to extend, but it is clear that this is a range.

It left abruptly, creating an unbalance. For this example, I'll utilize this level of demand. We do have an OB, so this is an OB, but let's just record the range itself, from high to low, so that as prices come in, we can see that there was a lot of momentum building up to this level. Although price is impulsive, pricing has thus far broken out of this bottom and is currently rebalancing the prior move. Therefore, on an LTF, we might wait for the price to stabilize, show us that they honestly want us to respect this region, and then actually go long from here to possibly return up to this highs.

Wicked

We can either categories it or dismiss it and continue because it hasn't held. Instead, search for bearish structure and consider going short. I won't go LTF and look at the entries for the following candle, but we can see that we wicked below it and then closed back up.

It depends on how it breaks—does it break abruptly or does it break in a corrective fashion with wicks—so in my perspective, this does not invalidate the demand zone. And as can be observed, it is obviously breaking with wicks.

This wick is an OB on LTF

Price came to test previous highs and test wick

Imbalance

This wick is an OB on LTF

As a result, when we obtain wicks on an LTF, if we do so on a 1h, it will be an OB. Wicks does nothing more than display OB on LTF. I won't therefore discuss the entrances on an LTF like the 5m or the 1m, but we can observe what follows. We acknowledge the demand zone and make corrections, but as you can see, as we break above it, we move up to test this wick, which is what we recognize to be an OB on an LTF. After that, we return to the prior highs before testing it again.

At that point, the price turns around once more. As a result, we may examine how the price relates to this wick, which is an OB on LTF as far as we are aware. We probably want the price to acquire liquidity before reverting, which is why we are currently wicking above it. However, in the end, it respects it, and we then return to the lowest rung. This pricing is current, but it simply reflects the concepts of purchasing to sell and selling to buy. Now that we have already entered this demand zone, prices are probably going to drop, and we can start hunting for sells.

5

SUPPLY AND DEMAND

Expansion and Consolidation

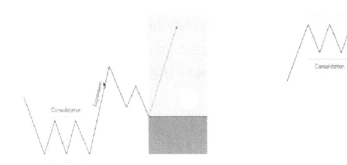

Price either grows or consolidates, depending on the market. Consolidation would be the corrective phase and expansion would be the impulsive phase because it is both impulsive and corrective.

Consolidation

Consolidation is a period of calm price movement in which the market trades inside the "dealing range".

When someone refers to a price as "range bound," "ranging," or "consolidating," they typically imply that it is merely moving horizontally rather than upward or downward.

The range can be tiny (with a spread of only a few dollars) or huge (with a spread from range high to range low of tens of thousands of dollars).

The timeline chosen will have an impact on this. Now, traditionally, the spread is looser the higher the timeframe, which generally means more money, and the spread is narrower the lower the timeframe, which means it may only be a few dollars.

A period of quiet, range-bound price movement, often known as sideways price action, characterizes the consolidation. As shown in the graphic below, the price is going sideways and not in a single direction but rather up, down, up, and down. This is the consolidation phase.

Market Expansion

A period of rapid price movement in either direction is known as a market expansion. When price makes an abrupt move to the upside or downside, it will provide us with large candle bodies or wicks. As may be seen in the picture above, we impulsively moved significantly higher. Since this involves expansion, we will see huge candles or wicks pointing in one way over the other.

Supply and Demand Theory

Demand zone (bullish price action): This is the region of consolidation before a sharp upward surge. Consequently, a demand zone is another name for a bullish consolidation block. A market that is in a range usually has bullish expansion after that. They can act as support when price movement drops into demand zones from the upper side. When starting or closing long or short positions, demand zones are utilized.

How should our demand zones be marked off?

We select the highest candle body and the lowest point of the range. Alternately, we may look at that price range as a whole.

Supply Zone: This is the period of consolidation before a sharp decline (bearish price action). A supply zone is often referred to as a bearish consolidation block.

A market that is in a range will typically be followed by bearish growth.

They may act as barrier when downward market action pushes up into supply zones. Supply zones are used to open short positions and/or close long positions.

How can our supply zones be marked off?

The wick serves as the range's highest point, and the lowest candle body serves as the range's true lowest point, which would be the lowest bodies rather than the wicks. However, I choose to consider the trading range's high and low together. However, in some instances where there is a large wick, we can use the candle body as a reference to locate the range without taking the size of the wick into account.

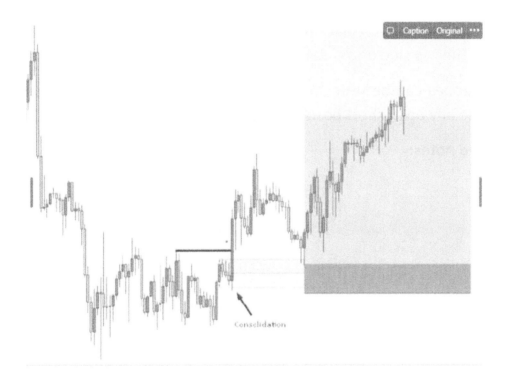

Let's continue now that we have an example of a demand zone. We observed an expansion following a consolidation that broke through a market that was range-bound and dragged the price back into it. So let's just focus on one instance. This range, which is also our consolidation range, was present. We'll just zoom in since it will be simpler to observe on an LTF with 4 candles present. Candles 1, 2, 3, and 4 are consolidating and moving in a sideways direction. The expansion happened on the next candle, which also caused the structure to collapse. You can see that after pressing up and producing an HH and HL, we then began to form these structures.

Demand

If we examine the demand rules, however:

1) The phase of consolidation that comes before a sudden uptick that also disturbs structural (bullish price activity).

2) Both the low of the range and the highest candle body may be employed. Or perhaps we should take into account that price range as a whole.

3) As soon as the expansion takes place, a demand zone is produced, shattering the framework. The top side of the demand will see price change.

4) Demand zones can be used to enter long positions. Additionally, we can use them to close any open short positions we may have.

Rules-related notes:

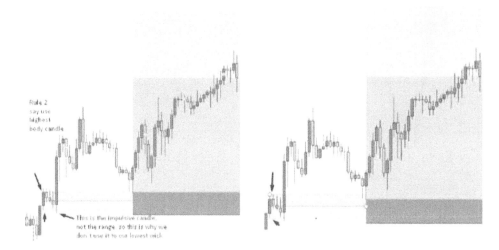

2) This blue candle would represent the low. Why else wouldn't the culprit be this wick? However, this candle was the only one that actually showed the expansion. The range was broken by this candle since it is the impulsive candle and not the range. The wick would be the lowest point, making it the lowest point. The highest candle body would represent the highest point, making it the high point. Rule 2 was also mentioned, though, alternatively we could take into account the entire trading range, which is what I personally do. So for me, the wick would be the lowest point and the highest point would be the candle.

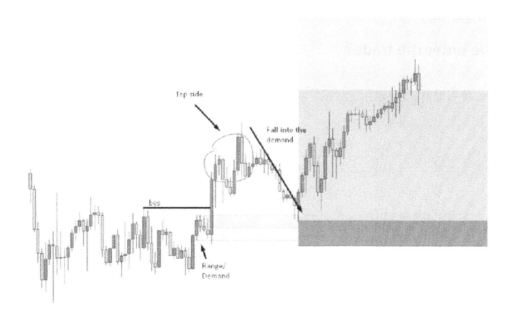

3) Break of structure, this is the range, this is our demand, so this is the top side, we fall back into demand

4) Because it is possible to see how someone responds to a request. Since we are confident that we will see the response, if we are thinking about selling moving forward, we should think about setting objectives or manually closing down once

we have witnessed how price responds to the level of demand and then wait for the upward surge.

How can we enter the trade?

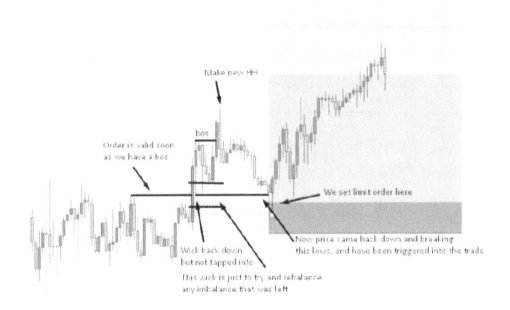

When we have a BOS, we can instantly put our entry at a limit order. As a result, following this BO, we can place a limit order at the top of the OB range. We can arrange entry at the top. We can see that we had wicked back down but would not have been hooked into the market because price has since been forced higher and formed a new HH.

This wick was placed here to try to balance out any imbalances that may have been left, but we also left imbalances in this location. If we hadn't pushed up HH and then dropped back down, breaking through these lows, we would have been triggered into the trade.

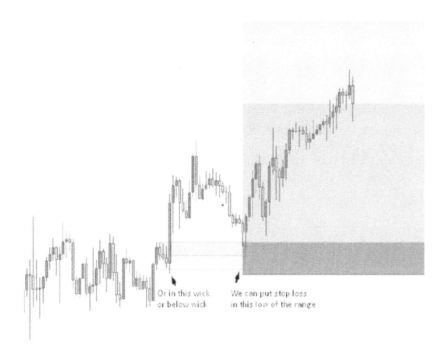

Or in this wick
or below wick

We can put stop loss
in this low of the range

We have two choices for our stop loss: we may put it at the low of the trade and range or we can consider any potential wicks. We can set our stop loss at that wick or below it before going forward because price declined to even out the entire sort of trading range and any imbalance or inefficiency that remained from this impulsive move (big candle that formed BOS).

Therefore, if we position our stop loss only at this type of block or trading region, it's conceivable that we will be tapped out with a wick before price goes further. It is therefore far safer to give ourselves a 1 to 2 pip buffer to account for the wick. But that serves as an example of a demand for which we are thinking about growth and consolidation, as well as other strategies.

Supply

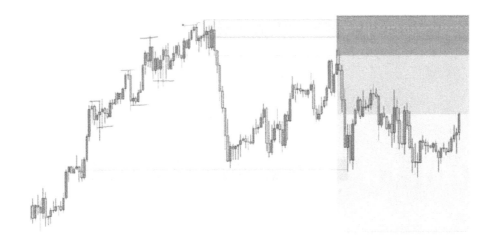

However, let's examine a supply example now. The first hour on GU has passed and we currently have a supply sample. As a consequence, we can see that adding the price to the HHs and HLs effectively rectified it. As a result, every one of these movements involves reaching highs, retracing, and moderating, then continuing after mitigating.

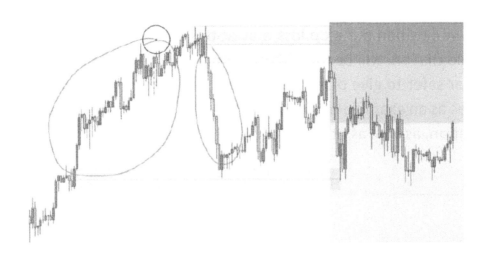

So, now that we're taking a closer look at this, we can see that we made a hasty move that negatively impacted the expansion. We can see that it is aggressive since the duration of the motion is the same while the size of the candles varies when we compare it to the entire move.

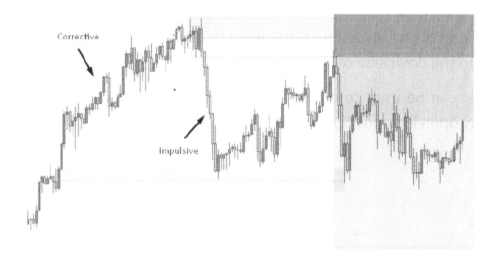

We have several candles within this, like these 2, but this move is impulsive and corrective to an extent of 80%

BOS is also present here and here on the downhill because we are in the expansion phase.

However, if we analyze the laws of supply:

The phase of consolidation that comes before a sudden downward movement (bearish price action). The low and high of the range are taken together. Alternately, we may look at that price range as a whole.

The supply zone is established first, followed by the expansion. The supply will be pushed up on the downside of the price action.

Supply zones can be used to enter shorts. Additionally, we can employ them to close out any open long positions.

1) There has been a bearish price movement. Where is the location of the previous range? This is it. The price reached this high, above which we had a low. It then climbed above the low but was unable to surpass it and establish a new high.

Instead, we observed two wicks, which showed that the upward rising momentum was somewhat waning. Once we have a small range and have identified the market, we can begin trading.

2) When we zoom in, where does the range start? Although it is corrective, this move is pushing up and it is the move that broke the high; as a result, it is not a range.

This is more of a range, so I'd be looking at where this bearish candle, or candle, might remain from here till the expansion begins. So, as you can see, we start with this wick and the lowest wick, which represent the highest and lowest points in the range, respectively. Because after the range-bound market consolidation, we begin the expansion.

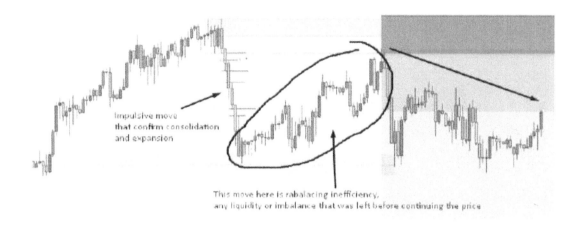

Impulsive move
that confirm consolidation
and expansion

This move here is rabalacing inefficiency,
any liquidity or imbalance that was left before continuing the price

3) This sharp decline supports a range expansion and consolidation. Therefore, any liquidity or imbalance that was left after this significant rise is being rebalanced before big banks continue to press the price lower, as I'm noting now. We are also rebalancing inefficiencies if we push back up.

What do we tap into here?

OB with imbalance left

See how price reacted to this zone

This line is equilibrium, the halfway point of OB

4) This paragraph highlights an important point. What are we drawing upon here? We expand by pushing downward, which came after consolidation. If we turn to the left, what do we see then? Demand zones: do they make sense? Due to our upward growth from a range.

We can look for long positions as the price starts to fall because we have taken advantage of a demand that has also produced an imbalance. And pay attention to how price has treated this region.

We already have this line because it suggests that the demand, or this OB, has reached halfway even if we prolong this longer. Along this line, the OB's equilibrium point can be found. Therefore, it has reached halfway.

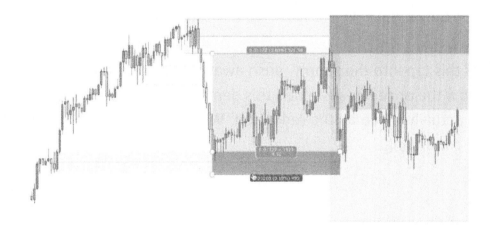

As we can see, price taps in. As a result of SnD levels, the balance is now much more revered. We tap in and push off, so certainly I'm not criticizing LTF if we were aiming for a long here; rather, I'm just illustrating the concepts underlying SnD. Therefore, we would enter at the top and set our stop loss immediately below.

Now that we are aware, we have this supply up here. We can either supply the base or see how it performs or we can target it right away. The price is 4.3RR right now, and the stop loss is 26 pip. Now, we can enter LTF with a stop loss that is significantly more restrictive than this.

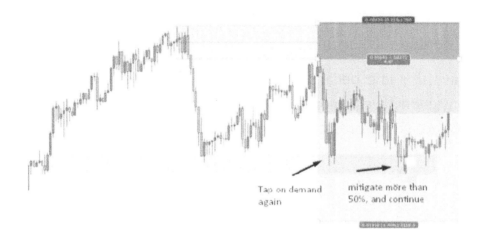

As a result of this tap into the supply, push away from, and return to this demand, we can see how the price has sustained this demand. We've admitted it, and in this instance, we actually made a 50% reduction. We actually cut to roughly 90% as a result before continuing.

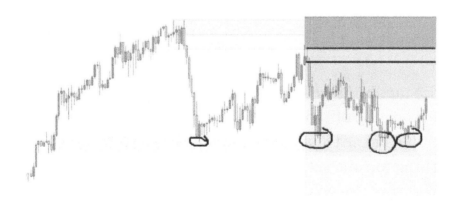

When we turn back to the supply, we can observe that it has grown as a result of consolidation. As we rebalance, we tap in, expecting to tap in to mitigate, and put our entry at the bottom of the range and our stop loss just above the high of the range by one or two pip(s).

Because of this, the price has been rebalanced and respects the supply zone; as a result, we are still looking for LLs while also keeping an eye on the demand zone/OB's position.

This might push up to another form of supply or a bearish OB up here given that this is the last upward movement before the downward movement that broke structure.

Made in the USA
Monee, IL
07 December 2024

72791242R00039